HELEN THAYER'S
ARCTIC ADVENTURE

A WOMAN AND A DOG WALK TO THE NORTH POLE

by Sally Isaacs   illustrated by Iva Sasheva

Few people have walked to the magnetic North Pole. Especially alone.

In 1988, Helen Thayer decided to try. She was 50 years old at the time. She planned to walk 585 kilometres (364 miles) around the magnetic North Pole.

No woman had ever done so before.

It took two years to research and train for the journey. To get her body ready, Helen ran, climbed and kayaked nearly every day. To get her mind ready, Helen spent five days alone in the Arctic.

Finally, Helen packed her clothes and supplies. She flew to a tiny village in northern Canada.

When Helen told a local bear hunter her plan, he protested.

'Don't go alone!' Tony warned. He worried about the fierce polar bears. 'You won't see them,' he said. 'They'll come to your tent while you sleep.'

But Helen wanted to go alone. She wasn't concerned that she might feel scared. She had climbed some of the highest mountains in the world. She had kayaked in the wildest rivers. She loved exploring the little-known corners of the world.

She had chosen the magnetic North Pole because that is the place to which all compasses point – the top of the world!

She was ready for this long, silent, solo journey.

'If you must go, take a team of dogs with you,' Tony begged.

But Helen refused. 'I want to depend on my own skills,' she said.

'Take just one dog,' Tony pleaded.

Helen bent down and stared into the dog's gentle face. He had no name because these dogs were not pets. They did not live inside the villagers' houses. They stood guard outside, tied to leads, ready to scare off polar bears.

Helen stroked the dog's ears. She agreed to take the dog. She named him Charlie.

Helen and Charlie started their journey over the wide-open frozen sea. Soon there were no sounds, except for their footsteps and the wind.

At night Helen set up her tent and crawled inside her sleeping bag.
She put Charlie outside the tent door to watch for polar bears.

On **DAY 5** Charlie and Helen were eating lunch near an iceberg. Suddenly Charlie stopped. He glared into the distance and growled. Helen's eyes followed Charlie's.

A full-grown bear was heading their way! Charlie burst forward until his lead stopped him. He snarled through his teeth.

Helen ripped off her skis. She placed her hand on the clip that attached Charlie to his lead.

The bear raced towards them. With a quick swipe of its paw, it tossed Helen's sledge into the air. Then the bear stood up on its hind legs, towering over the both of them.

Helen took a deep breath and grabbed her rifle. She had never intended to kill anything. But she had no choice. Helen fired at the bear's head. At the same time, the bear dropped down on all four legs, and the bullet sailed over its head. The bear stalked closer to Helen and Charlie.

Charlie snarled louder, and Helen unclipped his lead from his collar. He ran towards the bear and sank his teeth into its right rear heel.

The furious bear twisted round and round, trying to snatch Charlie, who held on with all his might. Helen grabbed her flare gun and fired flares at the ground in front of the bear, hoping to scare it off.

Finally, with a powerful shake, the bear tossed Charlie off its heel and ran away.

Charlie raced after the bear.

Helen was alone. Where was Charlie? Was he alive? What if he didn't return? How long should she wait for him?

Helen wanted to cry, but she didn't. She knew her tears would turn to icicles and burn her face.

Finally a tiny black dot came into view. It grew
larger. The dot turned into Charlie. He was back!

Helen and Charlie were becoming best friends. By the eighth night, an
exhausted Helen headed to her sleeping bag. There was Charlie! He
was sleeping inside the tent, his head resting on Helen's pillow. 'Well,
you left a corner of the pillow for my head,' she thought, smiling.

On **DAY 9** Helen woke to the sound of the wind slamming against her tent. A HUGE storm had blown in overnight.

Charlie was still sleeping. Helen bundled herself into her coat and tiptoed outside. The howling wind blasted ice and snow at her until she looked like a snowman.

She circled the tent and yanked down all the ropes to keep it secure. Then she scrambled back inside to where Charlie still slept.

'We're not going anywhere today, Charlie,' she said. Charlie raised his sleepy head. Of course, he had known that all along.

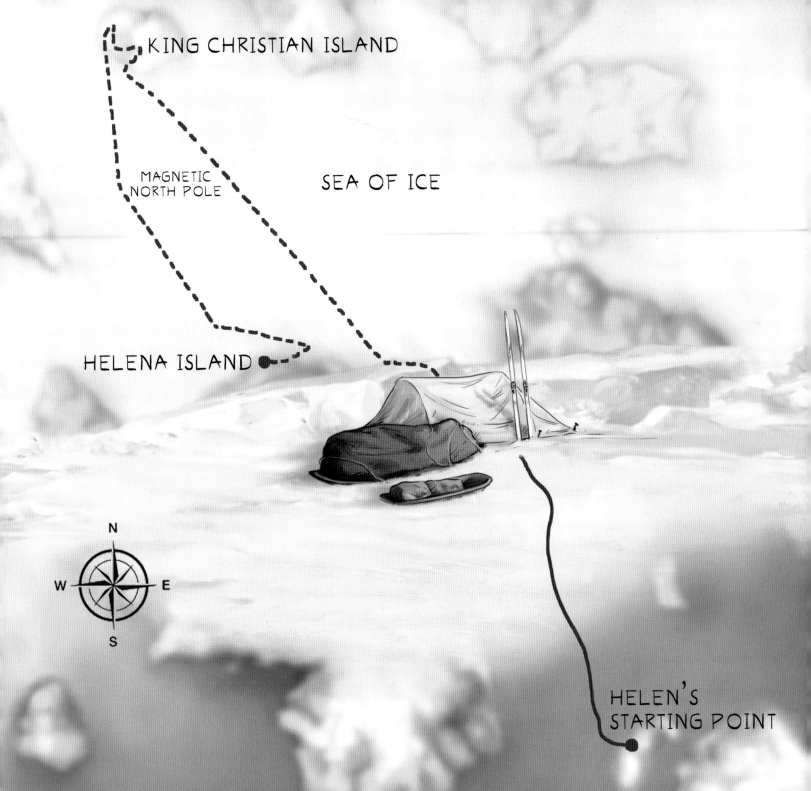

KING CHRISTIAN ISLAND

SEA OF ICE

MAGNETIC
NORTH POLE

HELENA ISLAND

N
W   E
S

HELEN'S
STARTING POINT

THEY WAITED.

ALL DAY.

ALL NIGHT.

Helen checked her map. There was such a long way to go.

As the sun rose, the wind still howled and the snow still pounded at the tent.

Helen had to decide:

Should they stay?

Should they move on?

Suddenly she heard a piercing sound outside.

CRACK!

Charlie jumped up. Helen did too. She peeked outside and gasped.

There was a long crack in the ice – only 1.5 metres (5 feet) from her tent door.

How could she leave? The violent wind was hurling ice and snow around.

How could she stay? The crack was moving towards her tent.

If the ice broke under the tent, they would fall into the icy black water.

HELEN DECIDED TO WAIT AGAIN.

ANOTHER DAY.

ANOTHER NIGHT.

Finally, the sun rose on a new day, and the wind settled down.
Helen and Charlie set off again for the North Pole.

Scary thoughts of cracked ice and polar bears swirled through
Helen's head as she took one careful step after another. She
bravely forced her fears away. *I can do this*, she thought.

And when she did, she would be the first woman
to walk alone to either of the Earth's poles.

So she and Charlie set off on their walk again.
And they walked and walked and walked.

By **DAY 20** the North Pole was getting closer. But Helen felt danger in the air. Dark clouds hung in front of her. The wind was chasing a wall of snow right at them. She skied – and Charlie ran – as fast as they could until she knew they must stop. The wind was ready to attack.

Helen grabbed her sack of ice screws and began hammering down the sledges, supplies and the end of Charlie's lead.

If she could make it to her sledge, she'd be able to protect herself by propping it up. But she didn't have time. She couldn't hide from the powerful wind. It knocked her down, and knocked off her goggles. Then, her body slid across the ice.

Helen picked herself up and looked around. Where was Charlie?

She spotted him behind the sledge. She dived in behind him.

Before she could catch her breath, Helen realized that she was hurt. She felt drops of blood above her right eye.

The ice had cut her eye. As the howling storm continued to smash into her, Helen had to be her own doctor. She yanked some string from from her hood. She tied a sweet wrapper over her eye like a patch. The string held it in place.

With her one good eye, Helen watched the wind sweep up the supplies and toss them away. Soon they were almost all gone!

All of Helen's food (except for a small bag of walnuts), most of the fuel for the stove and most of Charlie's food had blown away.

Helen counted the walnuts in her pocket. In order to have some food for the rest of the journey, she could eat just a small handful of nuts per day. Charlie would have to eat less too.

The storm took no pity on Helen. She was hurt and hungry. Her body shivered as it tried to warm up. The wind continued to pound her with ice and snow. As Helen lay beside Charlie she did maths problems in her head. That helped her keep her mind alert.

Hours passed. Finally the wind paused long enough for Helen to set up her tent. She dived inside and worried whether she could make it to the North Pole.

The next morning a quiet fog surrounded Helen's tent. She stood outside and checked the direction of the sun, the odometer on her sledge and her GPS. It was **DAY 21** and she was nearly there! She packed up, and she and Charlie walked on.

A few hours later, Helen checked her GPS again. She was at the North Pole!

Helen hugged Charlie and started the celebration she had planned for so long. She set up her camera and pulled three folded flags from her pack. She took pictures of herself, Charlie and the flags.

Then she unpacked the small metal container she had carried all the way to the North Pole. It held photos of her parents. There were also photos of herself and her husband on their wedding day.

She dug a small hole beneath the ice and buried the container. It would act as a sign that she had been here.

Helen got out her radio transmitter and announced to her friends in the village, 'I made it to the Pole today!'

Helen's friends made plans to send a plane to pick her up at a place that was smooth enough for landing. Helen counted the hours until she could head for home.

At last, on **DAY 27**, Helen heard the hum of an aeroplane, and she folded her tent for the last time.

The pilot landed the plane and helped Helen and Charlie aboard.

As the plane sailed into the sky, Helen looked out the window. She tried to find her tracks or her campsites. But there were no signs of her journey. The wind had already swept them away.

A Note from Helen Thayer

In 1988 I was the first woman to travel alone to the magnetic North Pole. I also became the first woman to travel alone to either of the world's Poles.

It was the most dangerous of all my expeditions because of the polar bears. I was successful because I took my time to plan and make sure that I had all of the right equipment and food.

Once I set out on skis pulling my own sledge, I kept going day after day, believing I would reach the Pole in spite of the polar bears and all the problems along the way. An important lesson I learned was that just one step at a time would get me there. I learned to always believe I would get there. I never allowed myself to think that I might not make it. It was a wonderful feeling to stand at the Pole and know that I had reached my goal.

When I returned I created Adventure Classroom. In this programme, I travel throughout the world to talk to children about my expeditions and how I reached my goals.

Helen Thayer

More About ...
HELEN THAYER

Helen Thayer was born in Whangerei, New Zealand, in 1937. Her parents taught her the joy of outdoor adventures. When she was in secondary school, her hero, Sir Edmund Hillary, came to speak to her class. He and his Sherpa guide, Tenzing Norgay, were the first humans to reach the world's highest peak, Mount Everest. Helen learned something from Hillary that day, and she believed it the rest of her life: "Anybody can be an explorer if they want to be ... Figure out what you want to do, and then go do it!"

Helen and Charlie met in the northern Canadian village of Resolute. A small plane flew them 92 kilometres (57 miles) up to Little Cornwallis Island where they began their walk. They walked through the Arctic from 30 March to 27 April, 1988, in a triangular route around the magnetic North Pole. She wrote a book about this historic journey. It is called *Polar Dream*. The expedition made Helen the first woman to walk alone to either of the Earth's poles.

Before going to the North Pole, Helen climbed to the top of some of the world's highest mountains: Mt McKinley in North America; Aconcagua in South America; Mt Cook in New Zealand; and Mt Lenin and Mt Communism in Tajikistan. She raced on skis, luges and in kayaks. After the North Pole adventure, she walked 1,005 kilometres (625 miles) alone in Antarctica, crossed the Sahara and Gobi deserts and kayaked through the Amazon rainforest.

Helen said at the end of *Polar Dream,* "When events become serious I feel a sense of excitement rather than despair. The solo journey to the Pole gave me a new awareness and greater confidence to push the limits of challenge. I quickly learned to acknowledge fear, know that it was all right to be afraid, and faced it squarely, confident that I would survive. That realization carried over into the rest of my life, and now gives me a quiet confidence that I can go on regardless of obstacles that might cross my path."

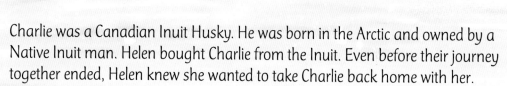

More About ...
CHARLIE

Charlie was a Canadian Inuit Husky. He was born in the Arctic and owned by a Native Inuit man. Helen bought Charlie from the Inuit. Even before their journey together ended, Helen knew she wanted to take Charlie back home with her.

For the first time in his life, Charlie rode in a car — from the airport in Vancouver, Canada, to Helen's home outside Seattle, USA. That is where he saw his first tree, his first garden and his first clump of wild flowers. Helen introduced him to his new family. The family consisted of Helen's husband, Bill, her cat, three dogs and seven goats.

In 1994 Charlie joined Helen and Bill on their 1,062-kilometre (660-mile) adventure in the Canadian Yukon. They lived beside a den of wild wolves while Helen and Bill studied the animal life. Charlie was able to communicate with the wolves and was quickly accepted into their pack.

Charlie lived to be 23 years old. He died in his sleep in 2003. He is buried near Helen and Bill's home, overlooking the mountains.

GLOSSARY

Arctic frozen area near the North Pole; very cold and wintry

expedition a long trip for a special purpose, such as exploring

fuel something that is burned to create heat, such as oil, gas or coal

GPS (Global Positioning System) a device that helps people follow a route to a place; Helen used an experimental GPS in the early days after its invention

iceberg a big mass of ice that is floating or frozen in the sea

ice screw a large screw that drills into ice, often used by climbers on frozen waterfalls, to hold ropes in place

magnetic North Pole a constantly moving large area in far northern Canada; all compasses point to the magnetic North Pole, but at the North Pole, a compass is useless

odometer something that measures distance traveled

radio transmitter something that sends and receives messages between distant places

supplies things needed for a task; Helen's supplies included a tent, map, stove, food, fuel, camera, compass and tools

FURTHER READING

Polar Regions (Explorer Travel Guides), Chris Oxlade (Raintree, 2013)

Powerful Polar Bears (Walk on the Wild Side), Charlotte Guillain (Raintree, 2013)

Secrets of the Polar Regions, Barbara Wilson (London Town Press, 2013)

WEBSITES

www.bbc.co.uk/education/topics/zkc4jxs
Learn about the polar regions and the life that lives there on this website full of fascinating videos.

www.discoveringthearctic.org.uk
The Royal Geographic Society have put this site together for children wanting to find out about all things arctic!

Critical thinking questions

1. Describe Charlie at the beginning of the book when Helen first met him. How was he different by the time he and Helen boarded the plane at the end of the story? What caused Charlie to become different?

2. Helen made many decisions during the story. What were they? How did Helen go about making her decisions? Would you have made the same choices she made? Explain your answer.

3. What did Helen do when she was afraid? Was she fearless, or did she just keep moving when she was afraid? Support your answer with details from the story.

INDEX

About the Author

Sally Isaacs was Editorial Director of Reader's Digest Educational Division before becoming a professional writer of nonfiction and educational books. She has written 50 books, including American history books, biographies and atlases for children. In 2004, her book *Cattle Trails and Cowboys* won the June Franklin Naylor Award for Best Book for Children on Texas History. Sally began her research on Helen Thayer's Arctic journey by reading Helen's book with its day-by-day accounts. She followed this with several telephone interviews with Helen. Sally is the co-founder and co-chair of the 21st Century Children's Nonfiction Conference.

About the Illustrator

Iva Sasheva is a master printmaker, painter, sculptor and book illustrator. Her first exhibition at the age of 13 was followed by a number of solo and group shows in Europe and America. As an artist she has contributed her work to more than 25 feature films and collaborated with authors in the creation of several graphic novels, literary novels and children's books.

Raintree is an imprint of Capstone Global Library Limited, a company incorporated in England and Wales having its registered office at 264 Banbury Road, Oxford OX2 7DY – Registered company number: 6695582

www.raintree.co.uk
myorders@raintree.co.uk

Editorial Credits
Michelle Bisson, editor; Ashlee Suker, designer; Nathan Gassman, Creative Director; Kathy McColley, production specialist

Photo Credits
Johanna Sturm, author photo; Helen Thayer, p. 26.

Printed and bound in China.
ISBN 978 1 4747 1065 7
19 18 17 16 15
10 9 8 7 6 5 4 3 2 1

British Library Cataloguing in Publication Data
A full catalogue record for this book is available from the British Library.